Commissioned by the Philharmonic Symphony Society of New

THE FIVE SACRED TREES
Concerto for Bassoon and Orchestra

Solo Bassoon with Piano Reduction

JOHN WILLIAMS

2nd Edition

ISBN 978-0-7935-5794-3

Unauthorized copying, arranging, adapting, recording or public performance
is an infringement of copyright. Infringers are liable under the law.
Visit Hal Leonard Online at
www.halleonard.com

7777 W. BLUEMOUND RD. P.O. BOX 13819 MILWAUKEE, WI 53213

THE FIVE SACRED TREES
Concerto for Bassoon and Orchestra

As we become increasingly aware of the damage done by the destruction of our forests, it is illuminating to discover that our ancestors, many thousands of years ago, prayed to the spirits before felling a tree. One prayer was appropriate for a maple, another for the elm, the ash and so on.

The English poet, Robert Graves, writes of these prayers, which I have been unable to find but which, nonetheless, have moved me to compose this music about trees featuring the bassoon, itself a tree.

This is all the result of a request for a concerto by the great bassoonist Judith Le Clair, whose unparalleled artistry is a mystery and a wonder in itself.

I

Eó Mugna, the great oak, whose roots extend to Connla's Well in the "otherworld," stands guard over what is the source of the River Shannon and the font of all wisdom. The well is probably the source of all music, too. The inspiration for this movement is the Irish Uilleann pipe, a distant ancestor of the bassoon, whose music evokes the spirit of Mugna and the sacred well.

II

Tortan is a tree that has been associated with witches and as a result, the fiddle appears, sawing away, as it is conjoined with the music of the bassoon. The Irish Bodhrán drum assists.

III

The *Tree of Ross* (or *Eó Rossa*) is a yew, and although the yew is often referred to as a symbol of death and destruction, the Tree of Ross is the subject of much rhapsodizing in the literature. It is referred to as "a mother's good," "Diadem of angels," and "faggot of the sages." Hence, the lyrical character of this movement, wherein the bassoon incants and is accompanied by the harp!

IV

Craeb Uisnig is an ash and has been described by Robert Graves as a source of strife. Thus, a ghostly battle, where all that is heard as the phantoms struggle, is the snapping of twigs on the forest floor.

V

Dathi, which purportedly exercised authority over the Poets, and was the last tree to fall, is the subject for the close of the piece. The bassoon soliloquizes as it ponders the secrets of the Trees.

John Williams

THE FIVE SACRED TREES
Concerto for Bassoon and Orchestra
(for Judith Le Clair)

JOHN WILLIAMS

I. Eó Mugna

Note: The clefs used in the Bassoon solo part appear differently from the solo line in the piano reduction.

© 1993 MARJER PUBLISHING
All Rights Reserved

II. Tortan

III. Eó Rossa

IV. Craeb Uisnig

24

V. Dathi

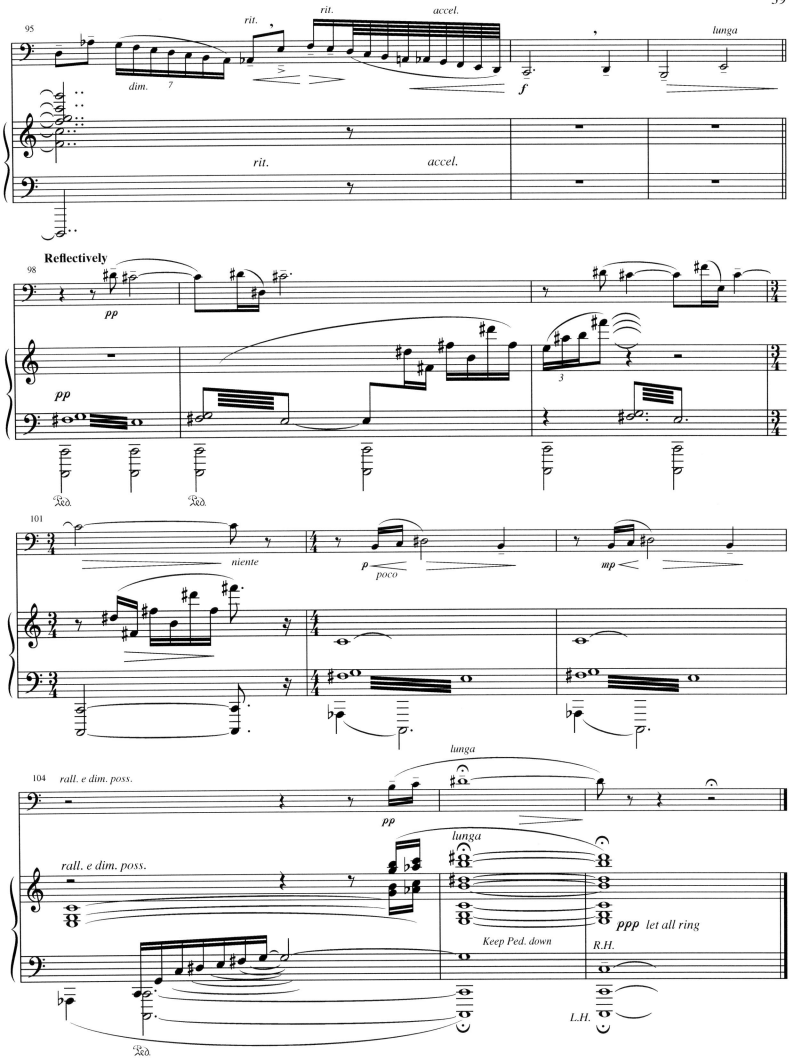